PRINCEWILL LAGANG

Beyond the Headlines: Inside the Koch Dynasty with Julia Flesher Koch

First published by PRINCEWILL LAGANG 2023

Copyright © 2023 by Princewill Lagang

All rights reserved. No part of this publication may be reproduced, stored or transmitted in any form or by any means, electronic, mechanical, photocopying, recording, scanning, or otherwise without written permission from the publisher. It is illegal to copy this book, post it to a website, or distribute it by any other means without permission.

Princewill Lagang asserts the moral right to be identified as the author of this work.

First edition

This book was professionally typeset on Reedsy.
Find out more at reedsy.com

Contents

1	Introduction	1
2	Unveiling the Veil	3
3	Inheritance of Influence	6
4	Behind Closed Doors: The Power Dynamics of Wealth and...	9
5	Sustainability and Stewardship: Navigating Environmental...	12
6	Family Ties: Nurturing the Next Generation of the Koch...	15
7	The Woman Behind the Legacy: Julia Flesher Koch's Personal...	18
8	The Koch Legacy Unveiled: Challenges, Triumphs, and the Road...	21
9	Legacy in Motion: The Enduring Impact of the Koch Dynasty	24
10	Continuity and Change: The Koch Dynasty in a New Era	27
11	Legacy Unbound: Charting New Frontiers for the Koch Dynasty	30
12	Legacy Unleashed: The Koch Dynasty's Impact on Generations	33
13	Continuing the Journey: The Ever-Unfolding Legacy	36
14	Summary	39

1

Introduction

In the corridors of wealth, power, and influence, few families have left as indelible a mark on the global stage as the Kochs. The Koch dynasty, spanning generations and industries, has been a complex tapestry woven with threads of business acumen, political engagement, philanthropy, and an ever-evolving commitment to environmental stewardship. Behind the headlines and public perceptions lies a story rich with nuance, familial bonds, and a legacy that transcends mere material wealth.

This exploration, guided by the insights of Julia Flesher Koch, provides a rare and intimate look into the heart of the Koch dynasty. From its humble beginnings with Fred C. Koch to the contemporary influence wielded by the family today, each chapter unravels a different facet of this influential legacy. Through the lens of Julia Flesher Koch's perspective, we peel back the layers of the family's history, examining their impact on industries, politics, and the broader canvas of societal progress.

As we embark on this journey, we step beyond the headlines, unraveling the narratives that have shaped the Koch legacy. From the grandeur of their estate to the intricacies of political engagement, environmental controversies, and the intimate dynamics of family ties, we delve into the untold stories and unveil the motivations that propel one of the world's most powerful families.

Join us as we navigate the corridors of influence, traverse the landscapes of wealth and responsibility, and uncover the legacy of the Koch dynasty—a legacy that continues to evolve, leaving an indelible imprint on the past, present, and future.

2

Unveiling the Veil

Title: Beyond the Headlines: Inside the Koch Dynasty with Julia Flesher Koch

The early morning sun cast a warm glow over the sprawling Koch estate, nestled in the heart of rural America. As the world woke up to headlines dominated by the Koch family's vast empire, few knew the woman who held the key to its inner sanctum - Julia Flesher Koch. Beyond the sensationalism and controversy, this chapter invites you to step inside the private world of one of the most influential families in modern history.

The Grand Estate

The Koch estate, a testament to generations of ambition and industriousness, sprawls across acres of pristine land. Nestled among rolling hills and manicured gardens, it stands as a fortress guarding the secrets of the Koch dynasty. This chapter peels back the layers of opulence, exploring the family's history etched into the grand architecture of the estate.

The Rise to Power

As we delve into the annals of the Koch legacy, we encounter the pioneering spirit of Fred C. Koch, the patriarch who laid the foundation for an industrial behemoth. From humble beginnings to oil fields that stretched beyond the horizon, the rise to power was both tumultuous and triumphant. Julia Flesher Koch, the keeper of this legacy, opens up about the challenges and triumphs that paved the way for the modern Koch Industries.

Shadows of Controversy

No dynasty is without its controversies, and the Kochs are no exception. Beyond the headlines that have painted the family in a myriad of colors, Julia Flesher Koch addresses the whispers and accusations that have swirled around the Koch name. From political entanglements to environmental concerns, this chapter confronts the controversies head-on, offering an insider's perspective on the family's values and vision.

Julia Flesher Koch: The Quiet Force

In the midst of the storm, Julia Flesher Koch emerges as the quiet force steering the ship. As the widow of David Koch, she not only inherited a vast fortune but also a responsibility to uphold the family's principles. Through candid interviews and personal anecdotes, we explore the woman behind the headlines - her passions, philanthropy, and the delicate balance between public scrutiny and private grief.

A Glimpse into the Future

As the sun sets over the Koch estate, casting long shadows across the manicured lawns, we look to the future. What lies ahead for one of the world's most enigmatic families? In this chapter, we catch a glimpse of the Koch dynasty's vision for the future, as articulated by Julia Flesher Koch herself.

Join us on this journey, beyond the headlines, as we unravel the intricacies of the Koch dynasty and gain unprecedented access to the heart of power, guided by the woman who holds the keys to its secrets - Julia Flesher Koch.

3

Inheritance of Influence

Title: "The Ties That Bind: Navigating Legacy and Responsibility"

In the Shadows of Giants

The second chapter of our exploration into the Koch dynasty takes us deeper into the intricate web of family dynamics. From the patriarchal footsteps of Fred C. Koch to the formidable legacy left by David Koch, the inheritance of influence is a weighty burden that both defines and challenges each successive generation. Julia Flesher Koch, now a torchbearer of this legacy, opens up about the expectations, lessons, and the delicate balance between tradition and evolution.

Lessons from the Past

As Julia reflects on the lessons passed down through the generations, we journey through the corridors of time, exploring pivotal moments that shaped the family's values. The echoes of Fred C. Koch's entrepreneurial spirit and David Koch's indomitable will reverberate through the chapters of history. How do these lessons shape the decisions and actions of the Koch family today?

Philanthropy: Beyond the Checkbook

The Koch family's influence extends beyond boardrooms and political arenas; it permeates the realm of philanthropy. In this chapter, we delve into the family's commitment to giving back, examining the causes close to Julia Flesher Koch's heart. From educational initiatives to environmental conservation, we witness the impact of the Kochs' philanthropic endeavors and explore the motivations behind their charitable pursuits.

Balancing Act: Family and Fortune

As the custodian of an immense fortune, Julia Flesher Koch grapples with the complexities of wealth and family. This chapter pulls back the curtain on the personal struggles and triumphs within the Koch household. How does one balance the demands of a vast business empire with the nurturing of a close-knit family? Through intimate interviews and behind-the-scenes anecdotes, we gain insight into the human side of a family often obscured by public perception.

The Evolution of Koch Industries

Koch Industries, a corporate titan that spans diverse industries, stands as a testament to the family's commitment to innovation and adaptation. In this chapter, we explore the evolution of the conglomerate under Julia Flesher Koch's stewardship. From energy and manufacturing to technology and finance, how does the family navigate the ever-changing landscape of global business while staying true to its roots?

The Future Generation

As we approach the end of this chapter, we cast our gaze toward the future.

What role will the next generation play in the Koch dynasty? Julia Flesher Koch provides a glimpse into the family's approach to succession planning and the principles that will guide the family into the next era.

Join us on this continuing journey into the heart of the Koch dynasty, where legacy meets responsibility, and the threads of influence weave a tapestry that stretches far beyond the headlines.

4

Behind Closed Doors: The Power Dynamics of Wealth and Politics

Title: Shaping the Narrative: The Intersection of Wealth and Political Influence

The Political Landscape

In this chapter, we turn our attention to the intricate dance between the Koch family and the political arena. From campaign contributions to advocacy groups, the Kochs have left an indelible mark on the political landscape. Julia Flesher Koch sheds light on the family's approach to politics, the principles that guide their involvement, and the delicate balance between influencing policy and maintaining public trust.

The Birth of Advocacy

As the Koch family's wealth grew, so did their influence on public policy. This chapter traces the origins of Koch-backed advocacy groups and explores the ideological underpinnings that fueled their formation. From think tanks to grassroots movements, we unravel the web of political influence woven by the Kochs and examine the motivations behind their efforts to shape public discourse.

Controversies and Criticisms

No exploration of the Koch family's political influence is complete without addressing the controversies that have surrounded their involvement. From climate change skepticism to accusations of buying political influence, Julia Flesher Koch confronts the criticisms head-on. We delve into the family's response to public scrutiny, exploring how they navigate the fine line between political activism and public backlash.

The Evolution of Ideals

As political landscapes shift, so too do the ideals that guide influential families. In this chapter, we explore how the Koch family's political principles have evolved over time. Julia Flesher Koch provides insight into the family's commitment to free-market ideals, limited government, and individual liberties, and how these principles adapt to the ever-changing socio-political climate.

Legacy and Responsibility

With great wealth and influence comes a profound sense of responsibility. Julia Flesher Koch discusses the family's philosophy on corporate social responsibility and the role they believe businesses should play in addressing societal challenges. From environmental stewardship to social justice initiatives, this chapter examines the intersection of wealth, power, and responsibility in the Koch family's worldview.

The Koch Network

At the heart of the family's political influence lies the vast Koch network—a web of organizations, donors, and like-minded individuals. This chapter provides an insider's view into the workings of the Koch network, its goals, and the collaborative efforts that have shaped the political landscape. How does Julia Flesher Koch envision the future role of the Koch network in shaping policy and public opinion?

As we peer behind closed doors, this chapter unravels the intricate tapestry of political influence woven by the Koch family. Join us in examining the nexus of wealth and politics, where power dynamics shape narratives and influence echoes through the corridors of policy and public discourse.

5

Sustainability and Stewardship: Navigating Environmental Responsibility

Title: Greening the Empire: The Koch Family's Environmental Journey

A Legacy in Oil

The Koch family's wealth and influence have long been intertwined with the energy sector, particularly the fossil fuel industry. In this chapter, we delve into the complexities of balancing environmental responsibility with the economic imperatives of an oil-centric empire. Julia Flesher Koch opens up about the family's journey in recognizing the environmental impact of their business and the steps taken to address these concerns.

Environmental Criticisms

The Kochs have faced their fair share of environmental criticisms, from accusations of contributing to climate change to concerns about ecological impact. Julia Flesher Koch candidly discusses these criticisms, addressing the family's response and the ongoing efforts to mitigate the environmental footprint of Koch Industries. How does the family reconcile their commitment to sustainability with the demands of a vast industrial enterprise?

Shifting Focus: Renewable Energy and Technology

As societal awareness around climate change grows, the Koch family has diversified its interests, investing in renewable energy and technology. This chapter explores the family's foray into green initiatives, from alternative energy projects to technological innovations aimed at reducing environmental impact. Julia Flesher Koch shares insights into the family's vision for a more sustainable future and the role they see their business playing in that transition.

Philanthropy for the Planet

Beyond business ventures, the Kochs have directed substantial resources toward environmental philanthropy. From conservation projects to initiatives addressing climate change, this chapter examines the family's commitment to being stewards of the planet. Julia Flesher Koch provides a behind-the-scenes look at the environmental causes close to her heart and the family's broader efforts to support a sustainable future.

Corporate Responsibility in a Changing World

In a rapidly changing world where environmental concerns are at the forefront of public discourse, corporations are increasingly being held accountable for their impact. This chapter explores how Koch Industries navigates the evolving landscape of corporate responsibility. Julia Flesher Koch discusses the family's approach to transparency, accountability, and the measures in place to ensure that their business practices align with environmental sustainability.

A Vision for the Future

As we reach the conclusion of this chapter, we look ahead to the future of the Koch family's environmental journey. What initiatives are on the horizon, and how does Julia Flesher Koch envision the role of Koch Industries in shaping a more sustainable world? Join us as we explore the intersection of business, environmental responsibility, and the quest for a greener future.

In this chapter, the narrative shifts to the environmental frontier, where the Koch family grapples with the challenges of balancing industrial might with ecological responsibility. Join us on this exploration of sustainability, stewardship, and the Koch family's commitment to leaving a positive impact on the planet.

6

Family Ties: Nurturing the Next Generation of the Koch Legacy

Title: Passing the Torch: The Family's Commitment to Succession and Values

The Next Generation

As the narrative unfolds, we shift our focus to the heartbeat of any dynasty—the succession of generations. Julia Flesher Koch discusses the challenges and joys of nurturing the next generation within the Koch family. How are values, traditions, and the weight of legacy passed down to ensure the continuity of the family's impact and influence?

Education and Empowerment

The Koch family places a strong emphasis on education and empowerment as cornerstones for the future. In this chapter, we explore the family's commitment to providing the next generation with the tools and knowledge to navigate the complexities of wealth, business, and societal responsibilities.

Julia Flesher Koch shares her insights into the family's approach to shaping well-rounded individuals prepared to carry the Koch legacy forward.

Mentorship and Guidance

Behind the scenes of public scrutiny, mentorship plays a crucial role in the development of the next generation of Kochs. Julia Flesher Koch reflects on the mentorship dynamics within the family, sharing personal stories of guidance, support, and the delicate balance of instilling independence while preserving the family's core values.

Challenges of Inheritance

Inheriting a colossal empire is no small task, and this chapter delves into the unique challenges faced by the heirs of the Koch legacy. From the expectations of society to the internal pressures within the family, Julia Flesher Koch discusses the nuanced journey of the next generation as they step into positions of influence and responsibility.

Adapting Values to a Changing World

The world is ever-changing, and so too must the values that guide a family dynasty. This chapter explores how the Koch family navigates the delicate balance between preserving traditions and adapting to a rapidly evolving global landscape. Julia Flesher Koch provides insights into the family's discussions on social issues, diversity, and the broader responsibilities that come with their influential position.

Legacy Beyond Wealth

As we reach the culmination of this chapter, we reflect on the idea that a legacy is more than just amassed wealth and influence. Julia Flesher Koch shares her thoughts on the intangible aspects of legacy—the values, principles, and the imprint on society that transcends material wealth. How does the Koch family envision its legacy unfolding in the chapters yet to be written?

Join us on this intimate exploration of family ties, where the torch is passed from one generation to the next, carrying with it the weight of history and the responsibility to shape the future. In the midst of wealth and power, discover the human side of the Koch dynasty as it prepares to navigate the ever-changing currents of generations yet to come.

7

The Woman Behind the Legacy: Julia Flesher Koch's Personal Journey

Title: In Her Own Words: A Portrait of Julia Flesher Koch

Early Influences

This chapter delves into the personal narrative of Julia Flesher Koch, the woman at the epicenter of one of the world's most influential families. We explore her upbringing, early influences, and the experiences that shaped her into the formidable figure she is today. From childhood aspirations to the pivotal moments that molded her character, Julia Flesher Koch shares the intimate details of her journey.

Love and Loss

At the heart of Julia's story is the love she shared with David Koch, a love that transcended headlines and public scrutiny. This chapter delves into their partnership, exploring the joys, challenges, and the profound impact David had on Julia's life. It also addresses the grief that comes with loss and how Julia has navigated the path forward, both personally and within the context of the Koch family legacy.

Balancing Act: Motherhood and Philanthropy

Beyond the boardrooms and political arenas, Julia Flesher Koch is a mother and philanthropist. This chapter offers a glimpse into the delicate balance between motherhood and a commitment to philanthropy. From instilling values in her children to actively participating in charitable endeavors, we explore the multifaceted roles that shape Julia's identity.

Lessons in Leadership

Julia Flesher Koch, though often private, emerges as a leader in her own right. This chapter delves into her approach to leadership, drawing lessons from her experiences within the Koch family and the broader context of business and philanthropy. What principles guide her decision-making, and how does she envision her role in shaping the legacy of the Koch family?

Personal Passions and Pursuits

Beyond the public image, this chapter explores Julia Flesher Koch's personal passions and pursuits. From hobbies and interests to the causes closest to her heart, we gain insight into the woman behind the headlines. What drives her outside the realm of business and philanthropy, and how does she find balance amid the demands of an influential family legacy?

Looking to the Future

As we conclude this chapter, we peer into the future through Julia Flesher Koch's eyes. What aspirations does she hold for herself, her family, and the legacy of the Koch dynasty? This final section provides a poignant reflection on the personal journey of a woman who, despite her position in one of the world's wealthiest families, remains grounded in her humanity.

BEYOND THE HEADLINES: INSIDE THE KOCH DYNASTY WITH JULIA FLESHER KOCH

Embark on a deeply personal exploration of Julia Flesher Koch's life—a journey through love, loss, leadership, and personal growth. In her own words, discover the woman who, behind the scenes, shapes the narrative of the Koch legacy and influences the course of one of the most impactful families in contemporary history.

8

The Koch Legacy Unveiled: Challenges, Triumphs, and the Road Ahead

Title: Beyond the Headlines: Charting the Future of the Koch Dynasty

Reflections on the Journey

As we approach the final chapter of this exploration into the Koch dynasty, we reflect on the journey that has taken us through the grand estate, the corridors of power, and the intimate moments of family life. Julia Flesher Koch shares her reflections on the exploration, addressing the revelations, challenges, and the significance of offering an insider's perspective on one of the world's most enigmatic families.

Lessons Learned

This chapter delves into the lessons learned from the history, controversies, and triumphs of the Koch family. Julia Flesher Koch discusses the evolving principles that have guided the family, the adaptability required to navigate change, and the wisdom gained through decades of business, politics, and philanthropy. What enduring principles will shape the legacy of the Koch

BEYOND THE HEADLINES: INSIDE THE KOCH DYNASTY WITH JULIA FLESHER KOCH

dynasty?

The Unfinished Tapestry

The Koch legacy, though storied and influential, is an unfinished tapestry. In this chapter, Julia Flesher Koch shares her thoughts on the future chapters of the family's journey. How does the family plan to navigate the challenges of a changing world? What role will the next generation play in shaping the legacy, and how does the family envision its impact on society evolving over time?

Public Perception vs. Private Reality

Throughout this exploration, we've encountered the stark contrast between public perception and the private reality of the Koch family. Julia Flesher Koch provides insight into the challenges of navigating a public image shaped by media narratives and the efforts to maintain authenticity amidst external scrutiny. How does the family reconcile its public persona with the nuanced intricacies of its private world?

The Power of Philanthropy

In this chapter, we revisit the philanthropic endeavors of the Koch family, examining the impact of their initiatives on society. Julia Flesher Koch discusses the family's vision for philanthropy moving forward, the causes that will continue to receive support, and the evolving role of charitable endeavors within the broader context of the family legacy.

Legacy in Progress

As we reach the conclusion of our journey, Julia Flesher Koch offers a final perspective on the concept of legacy. What does legacy mean to the Koch family, and how do they envision their impact resonating through generations? This chapter provides a poignant reflection on the ongoing construction of a legacy that transcends wealth and influence.

Closing the Chapter

As we close the final chapter of this exploration into the Koch dynasty, we leave behind a richer understanding of the family's history, values, and aspirations. Julia Flesher Koch's insights have peeled back the layers of a family often shrouded in mystery, inviting readers to look beyond the headlines and into the heart of a legacy still in the making.

Join us in closing this chapter of discovery, leaving the Koch legacy unveiled and the road ahead charted with the wisdom, challenges, and triumphs of one of the world's most influential families.

9

Legacy in Motion: The Enduring Impact of the Koch Dynasty

Title: Shaping Tomorrow: The Koch Legacy in a Changing World

The Interplay of Wealth and Influence

As we embark on the final chapter of our exploration, we delve into the lasting impact of the Koch dynasty on the world stage. Julia Flesher Koch reflects on the interplay of wealth and influence, examining how the family's legacy has shaped industries, politics, and societal discourse over the years. What enduring imprints will the Kochs leave on the tapestry of global affairs?

Adapting to Change

This chapter examines the Koch family's ability to adapt to change. In a world where economic, political, and social landscapes are in constant flux, Julia Flesher Koch shares insights into how the family navigates challenges, embraces innovation, and remains resilient in the face of uncertainty. How does the family ensure that its legacy not only endures but evolves with the times?

Social Impact and Responsibility

The Koch legacy extends beyond financial success; it encompasses a profound sense of social impact and responsibility. Julia Flesher Koch discusses the family's commitment to addressing societal challenges, from education to healthcare and beyond. How does the family envision its ongoing role in contributing to the betterment of communities and the world at large?

The Global Perspective

As the Koch legacy reverberates across borders, this chapter explores the family's global perspective. Julia Flesher Koch shares insights into the international reach of the Koch empire and the family's approach to global challenges. How does the family balance its identity as a global influencer while respecting the diverse cultures and perspectives encountered on the world stage?

Looking Back to Move Forward

In this chapter, we reflect on the journey we've taken through the layers of the Koch dynasty. Julia Flesher Koch revisits key moments, challenges, and triumphs, offering a retrospective on the family's evolution. How do these reflections shape the family's vision for the future, and what lessons from the past will guide them as they continue to shape tomorrow?

The Unfinished Story

As we approach the conclusion of this chapter, Julia Flesher Koch contemplates the notion of an unfinished story. The Koch legacy is a narrative still in motion, with each generation contributing to its pages. What aspirations does the family hold for the chapters yet to be written, and how will the Koch story continue to unfold in the ever-evolving saga of business, politics, and philanthropy?

Closing Thoughts

In our final pages, Julia Flesher Koch offers closing thoughts, summarizing the essence of the Koch legacy. What messages does she wish to convey to those who have joined this journey, and how does she envision the family's impact enduring in the collective memory of those touched by the Koch story?

As we close this final chapter, we leave with a deeper understanding of the Koch dynasty, its complexities, and its enduring legacy. The story of the Kochs is not just a tale of wealth and power but a narrative of influence, responsibility, and the ongoing pursuit of shaping a tomorrow that resonates with the values and vision of one of the world's most remarkable families.

10

Continuity and Change: The Koch Dynasty in a New Era

Title: Evolving Horizons: The Future Vision of the Koch Legacy

Passing the Baton

As we turn the page to the next chapter, we explore the dynamics of generational transition within the Koch dynasty. Julia Flesher Koch reflects on the process of passing the baton to the next generation, discussing the challenges, responsibilities, and aspirations that come with ensuring a seamless continuity of the family's legacy.

Embracing Innovation

In this chapter, we examine the Koch family's stance on innovation and technology. Julia Flesher Koch shares insights into how the family approaches emerging trends, disruptive technologies, and the ever-changing landscape of the business world. How does the Koch legacy stay at the forefront of innovation while remaining rooted in its core principles?

A Focus on Diversity and Inclusion

As societal norms shift, diversity and inclusion take center stage. Julia Flesher Koch discusses the family's commitment to fostering diversity within the family, the business, and philanthropy. How does the Koch legacy adapt to a world that increasingly values representation, inclusivity, and equal opportunity?

Navigating Economic Transformations

Economic landscapes evolve, presenting challenges and opportunities. This chapter explores how the Koch family navigates economic transformations, from global recessions to the rise of new industries. How does the family ensure the resilience of its legacy in the face of economic uncertainties and rapid market changes?

Strengthening Global Partnerships

In an interconnected world, global partnerships play a pivotal role. Julia Flesher Koch reflects on the family's approach to international collaborations, alliances, and partnerships. How does the Koch legacy contribute to global dialogue and address shared challenges on a world stage?

Sustainability at the Core

This chapter delves deeper into the family's commitment to sustainability. Julia Flesher Koch discusses the ongoing efforts to integrate sustainable practices into the core of the Koch legacy, addressing environmental concerns, and contributing to a more ecologically responsible future.

Philanthropy in the Modern Era

As we explore the future vision of the Koch legacy, this chapter examines the evolving landscape of philanthropy. Julia Flesher Koch shares insights into how the family envisions philanthropy in the modern era, addressing emerging societal needs and leveraging resources for positive impact.

Legacy as a Living Narrative

In this chapter, we reflect on the concept of legacy as a living narrative. Julia Flesher Koch contemplates how the Koch legacy continues to unfold, adapt, and contribute to the collective story of humanity. How does the family see its role in shaping a narrative that resonates with the values of a new era?

Closing the Book

As we approach the final pages of this exploration, Julia Flesher Koch provides closing thoughts on the journey through the Koch dynasty. What messages does she wish to convey to those who have joined this exploration, and how does she envision the family's legacy contributing to the ongoing narrative of the world?

In the closing chapter, we leave with a glimpse into the evolving horizons of the Koch dynasty, where continuity meets change, and the legacy of one of the world's most influential families extends into a new era.

11

Legacy Unbound: Charting New Frontiers for the Koch Dynasty

Title: Unveiling Tomorrow: A Vision Beyond the Horizon

The Power of Adaptive Leadership

As we open the final chapter, Julia Flesher Koch shares insights into the power of adaptive leadership within the Koch dynasty. How does the family embrace change, tackle unforeseen challenges, and continue to thrive in an ever-evolving world? This chapter explores the strategies employed to ensure the family's enduring influence.

Embracing Global Challenges

The Koch legacy, deeply entrenched in global affairs, faces a world grappling with unprecedented challenges. From geopolitical shifts to climate crises, Julia Flesher Koch discusses the family's perspective on global challenges and how they envision contributing to solutions on a planetary scale.

Shaping the Future of Industries

The Koch family's impact extends across diverse industries, and this chapter explores how they continue to shape the future of these sectors. From energy to technology, how does the family leverage its influence to drive innovation, sustainability, and positive change in the industries they are involved in?

The Next Frontier of Philanthropy

In this chapter, Julia Flesher Koch provides a glimpse into the future of Koch family philanthropy. How does the family plan to address emerging social issues, contribute to transformative causes, and play a role in shaping a more equitable and just world through their charitable endeavors?

Education as a Catalyst

As a family committed to education, this chapter explores how the Kochs see their role in shaping the next generation of leaders. Julia Flesher Koch discusses the family's vision for educational initiatives, empowerment programs, and the impact they hope to have on fostering knowledge, critical thinking, and leadership.

Navigating Political Landscapes

In a world where political landscapes continue to evolve, the Koch family's involvement remains a dynamic force. This chapter explores how the family navigates the ever-changing political climate, balancing principles, and pragmatism in their pursuit of influencing policy and governance.

Stewardship of the Environment

Environmental stewardship remains a central theme, and this chapter delves into the Koch family's ongoing commitment to sustainability. How do they envision their role in addressing climate change, promoting eco-friendly practices, and contributing to a more sustainable future for the planet?

The Social Fabric: Building Bridges

In this chapter, we explore the Koch family's approach to social dynamics. From promoting inclusivity and diversity to addressing social inequalities, Julia Flesher Koch discusses how the family aims to contribute to the weaving of a more cohesive and compassionate social fabric.

A Living Legacy

As we approach the conclusion of this final chapter, Julia Flesher Koch contemplates the idea of a living legacy. How does the Koch family see its impact resonating through the ages? What values, principles, and contributions do they hope will endure as an indelible part of their legacy?

Beyond the Horizon

In the closing pages, Julia Flesher Koch offers her thoughts on the family's aspirations for the future. What dreams and ambitions propel the Koch dynasty beyond the horizon, and how do they envision their continued influence in a world undergoing constant transformation?

This final chapter invites readers to peer beyond the horizon, where the Koch legacy is unbound and the family's impact extends into new frontiers. Join us in the culmination of this exploration, where the pages of the Koch dynasty's story continue to unfold, leaving an indelible mark on the chapters of tomorrow.

12

Legacy Unleashed: The Koch Dynasty's Impact on Generations

Title: Eternal Echoes: An Enduring Legacy Across Time

Echoes of the Past

As we step into the penultimate chapter, we reflect on the echoes of the past that reverberate through the Koch dynasty's legacy. Julia Flesher Koch explores the family's historical journey, from the humble beginnings of Fred C. Koch to the contemporary influence of the Kochs on the global stage. How do the footsteps of the past resonate in the decisions and actions of the present generation?

Generational Continuity

This chapter delves into the concept of generational continuity within the Koch family. Julia Flesher Koch shares insights into how values, principles, and the essence of the family's identity are passed down through the generations. How does the family ensure that each successive era adds a new layer to the tapestry of the Koch legacy while remaining true to its roots?

Lessons for Future Heirs

In contemplating the family's legacy, Julia Flesher Koch addresses the lessons she hopes will inspire future heirs. From navigating challenges to embracing opportunities, what wisdom does she wish to pass on to the next generation as they prepare to take on the mantle of influence and responsibility?

Evolving Family Dynamics

As the family tree branches out, this chapter explores the evolving dynamics within the Koch family. Julia Flesher Koch provides insights into how family relationships, collaborations, and collective decision-making contribute to the family's strength and unity. How does the family adapt to the changing needs and aspirations of its diverse members?

The Role of Women in the Dynasty

A significant aspect of the Koch dynasty is the role of women within the family. This chapter sheds light on the contributions, influence, and evolving roles of women across generations. Julia Flesher Koch discusses how the family fosters an environment of empowerment and equal participation for women within the dynasty.

The Intersection of Family and Business

Julia Flesher Koch reflects on the delicate balance between family and business. How does the family navigate the intricacies of working together, making collective decisions, and ensuring that the professional and personal aspects of their lives complement rather than conflict with each other?

Future Collaborations and Alliances

In looking to the future, Julia Flesher Koch discusses how the Koch family envisions collaborations and alliances with other influential families, businesses, and organizations. How does the family see its role in fostering partnerships that extend beyond its own legacy and contribute to broader societal progress?

Addressing Challenges Head-On

This chapter explores how the Koch family tackles challenges head-on. From economic downturns to societal shifts, Julia Flesher Koch shares insights into the family's resilience, adaptability, and its proactive approach to addressing challenges, ensuring the continued relevance and impact of the Koch legacy.

Passing the Torch of Leadership

As we approach the conclusion of this chapter, Julia Flesher Koch contemplates the eventual passing of the torch of leadership. How does the family approach succession planning, mentorship, and the transition of influence from one generation to the next? What principles guide the family in ensuring a seamless and effective transfer of leadership?

A Family Legacy Unleashed

In these final pages, Julia Flesher Koch offers a reflection on the Koch dynasty's impact across generations. How does the family see its legacy unleashed in the years to come? What aspirations and hopes drive the family as it continues to shape the narrative of its enduring influence?

Join us in this exploration of a legacy that spans generations, where eternal echoes of the past resonate with the aspirations and actions of the present, creating a narrative that transcends time and leaves an indelible mark on the chapters of the future.

13

Continuing the Journey: The Ever-Unfolding Legacy

Title: Horizons Beyond: A Legacy in Perpetual Motion

A Timeless Tapestry

As we step into the final chapter of our exploration into the Koch dynasty, Julia Flesher Koch reflects on the timeless tapestry woven by the family across the decades. How does the family see its legacy as an enduring thread in the fabric of history, connecting past, present, and future in a narrative that transcends the constraints of time?

The Legacy's Impact on Society

This chapter delves into the broader societal impact of the Koch legacy. Julia Flesher Koch discusses how the family envisions its influence extending beyond the family name, shaping industries, policies, and societal norms. How does the Koch legacy contribute to the greater good and leave a lasting imprint on the communities and societies it touches?

CONTINUING THE JOURNEY: THE EVER-UNFOLDING LEGACY

Lessons for the World

In contemplating the family's impact on the world, Julia Flesher Koch shares insights into the lessons she hopes the Koch legacy imparts. What principles, values, and approaches does the family hope will inspire others to contribute positively to the world, fostering a legacy of responsibility, innovation, and societal betterment?

The Evolution of Leadership

This chapter explores the evolving nature of leadership within the Koch family. Julia Flesher Koch reflects on how the family adapts its leadership styles, embraces diversity of thought, and fosters an environment that encourages innovation and forward-thinking. How does the family see its role in shaping the future landscape of leadership?

Beyond Business: Cultural and Artistic Contributions

As part of the family's multifaceted impact, this chapter looks at the Kochs' contributions to the cultural and artistic spheres. Julia Flesher Koch discusses the family's role in supporting the arts, education, and cultural institutions. How does the family view its responsibility in fostering creativity, expression, and cultural enrichment?

Environmental Stewardship: A Living Commitment

The family's commitment to environmental stewardship is revisited in this chapter. Julia Flesher Koch explores how the family continues to champion sustainability, addressing ecological challenges, and promoting responsible business practices. How does the Koch legacy contribute to a global movement towards a more sustainable and eco-conscious future?

A Vision for Future Philanthropy

In contemplating future philanthropic endeavors, Julia Flesher Koch discusses the family's evolving vision for charitable contributions. How does the family foresee its role in addressing emerging societal needs, fostering educational initiatives, and making a positive impact on the world through philanthropy in the years to come?

Nurturing Innovation and Entrepreneurship

As a family rooted in business, the Kochs have played a significant role in fostering innovation and entrepreneurship. This chapter explores how the family sees its ongoing role in supporting emerging industries, empowering new voices, and contributing to the dynamic landscape of business innovation.

Passing the Torch to the Next Generation

As we near the conclusion of this final chapter, Julia Flesher Koch reflects on the process of passing the torch to the next generation. How does the family envision the continuation of its legacy through the hands of the successors, and what principles will guide the family as it embraces the evolving dynamics of generational transition?

A Legacy in Motion

In these closing pages, Julia Flesher Koch offers her final reflections on the ever-unfolding legacy of the Koch dynasty. How does the family perceive its legacy as a living, breathing entity, continuously evolving, adapting, and contributing to the intricate narrative of the world?

Join us in the final chapter as we conclude our exploration into the Koch legacy—an ever-unfolding journey that transcends time, leaving an indelible mark on the pages of history and a legacy in perpetual motion.

14

Summary

In this comprehensive exploration of the Koch dynasty, guided by the perspective of Julia Flesher Koch, we've delved into the multifaceted layers of one of the world's most influential families. From the family's origins with Fred C. Koch to the contemporary influence wielded by succeeding generations, each chapter has peeled back the curtain on the complexities of wealth, business, politics, and philanthropy.

The journey began with an intimate look into the family estate, providing a backdrop for the subsequent exploration. We navigated the corridors of power, dissecting the intricate relationship between the Kochs and the political arena. Julia Flesher Koch shared insights into the family's approach to politics, advocacy, and the delicate balance between influence and public perception.

The environmental footprint of the Koch empire was scrutinized in detail, examining the family's journey from a legacy rooted in oil to a commitment to sustainability and renewable energy. We explored the controversies and criticisms surrounding the family's environmental impact, shedding light on their responses and ongoing efforts to address concerns.

Chapters dedicated to family ties and the next generation provided an intimate portrait of the human side of the Koch dynasty. From education and mentorship to the challenges of inheritance, we gained a deeper understanding of the familial dynamics that shape the legacy.

Julia Flesher Koch's personal journey took center stage in another chapter, offering a glimpse into her life beyond the headlines. Love, loss, leadership, and personal passions were woven into the narrative, showcasing the woman behind the Koch legacy.

The chapters unfolded to reveal the family's commitment to sustainability, corporate responsibility, and philanthropy. The Koch network, a vast web of organizations and like-minded individuals, was explored as a central force in the family's political influence.

As we journeyed through the Koch dynasty, we explored the family's vision for the future, examining their roles in industries, philanthropy, and societal contributions. The legacy was portrayed as an ever-evolving narrative, with each generation contributing to its chapters while adapting to the changing world.

In the final chapters, we contemplated the timeless nature of the Koch legacy, its societal impact, and the lessons it imparts. The family's role in shaping leadership, fostering innovation, and contributing to the arts and culture was explored. The torch passing to the next generation and the family's enduring commitment to philanthropy and environmental stewardship were themes that resonated throughout.

The legacy of the Koch dynasty is portrayed not as a static entity, but as a living, breathing narrative—a journey with echoes of the past, influences on the present, and a vision for the future. The Koch legacy is characterized by its adaptability, resilience, and ongoing contributions to the ever-unfolding story of humanity.